Learning the Violin

Book One

For individual study, single-string classes, or mixed-string classes

expanded edition

by Cassia Harvey

CHP280

C. Harvey Publications

www.charveypublications.com

Warmup Exercise for the Beginning of Class

0 1 2 3 4 3 2 1

0 1 2 3 4 3 2 1

0 1 2 3 4 3 2 1

0 1 2 3 4 3 2 1

0

Play this exercise on all four strings.
Use it as a warmup every time you play.

1. Parts of the Violin and Bow

VIOLIN

Chinrest or sponge
goes here.

1. scroll
2. peg box
3. pegs
4. nut
5. neck
6. fingerboard
7. sides
8. f holes
9. bridge
10. tailpiece
11. fine tuners

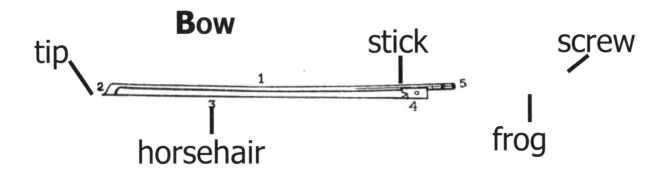

2. Taking care of the Violin

Keep your violin away from pets.

Don't let the violin drop (or the bow).

The wood is very fragile.

No water on the violin or bow.

Keep the violin off of heaters and away from open windows.

3. Taking care of the Bow

Don't touch the bow hair!

Righty-tighty: To tighten the bow, turn the screw to the right.

Lefty-loosey: To loosen the bow, turn the screw to the left.

Always loosen the bow when you are finished playing.

Keep the violin and bow up off the floor.

4. The Open Strings

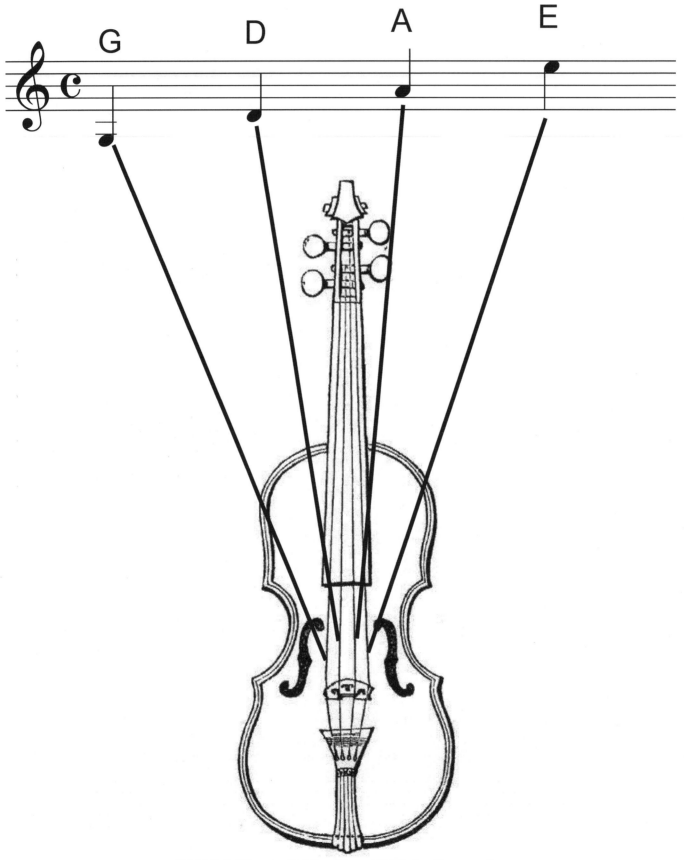

5. Pluck the Open Strings
(Lowest to Highest)

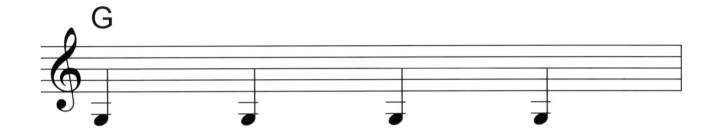

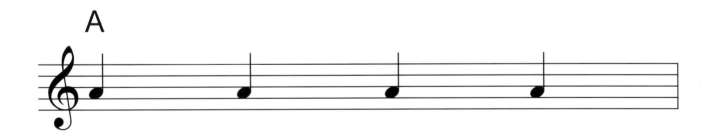

6. Open String Song

play with long bows, from the frog to the tip

GGGG   DDDD   AAAA   EEEE

EEEE   AAAA   DDDD   GGGG

GG DD AA EE EE AA DD GG

GDGD   DADA   AEAE   EADG

7. Mississippi Hot Dog

4 short bows and 2 long bows

Play the rhythm "Mississippi Hot Dog"
on each note:

G G D D   A A E E

G D A E   E A D G

G D   D A   A E   E A

8. Blueberry Song:
Long-Short-Short

G - GG   G - GG

D - DD   D - DD

A - AA   A - AA

E - EE   E - EE

A - AA   A - AA

D - DD   D - DD

9. Speedy Open Strings

AAAA EEEE

AAAA DDDD

GGGG DDDD

AAEE AAEE

AADD AADD

GGDD GGDD

10. The Finger Numbers

Using the Fingers

0 is for open string
1 is for first finger
2 is for second finger
3 is for third finger
4 is for fourth finger
The thumb goes under the neck of the violin.

11. First Finger Song

0000   1111   0000   1111

00   11   00   11   1111   0000

String Class: Play on the
A string or the D string.
Solo: Can be played on all
4 strings.

12. First Finger Challenge

0011   0011   0000   1111

0011   1100   1111   0000

0101   0000   0101   0000

13. Second Finger Song

0000   1111   2222   1111

0000   1111   2222   1111

00 11 22 11 00 11 22 11 00

String Class: Play on the
A string or the D string.
Solo: Can be played on all
4 strings.

14. Second Finger Challenge!

11 00   11 22   11 22 1111

22 11   2121   2121   0000

15. Hot Cross Buns

210 -   210 -

0000 1111

210 -

String Class: Play on the
A string or the D string.
Solo: Can be played on all
4 strings.

16. Au clair de la Lune

0001   2 - 1 -   0211   0 ---

0001   2 - 1 -   0211   0 ---

17. Mary Had a Little Lamb

2 1 0 1

2 2 2 -

1 1 1 -

2 2 2 -

2 1 0 1

2 2 2 2

1 1 2 1

0 - - -

String Class: Play on the A string or the D string. Solo: Can be played on all 4 strings.

18. Third Finger Song

0000   1111   2222   3333

2222   3333   2222   1111

00 11 22 33 22 33 22 11 00

String Class: Play on the
A string or the D string.
Solo: Can be played on all
4 strings.

19. Third Finger Challenge!

11 22 33 22 11 22 33 22

22 33 21 21 00 11 23 23

20. Finger Training

0 1 2 3   4 3 4 3

4 3 2 1   0 1 0 1

0 1 2 3   4 3 4 3

4 3 2 1   0 1 0 1

2 3 2 3   2 1 2 1   0

String Class: Play on the
D string.
Solo: Can be played on all
4 strings.

21a. Ode to Joy

String Class: Start on the D string.   Beethoven
     Solo: Start on the A string.

2 2 3 4 4 3 2 1

0 0 1 2 2 1 1 -

2 2 3 4 4 3 2 1

0 0 1 2 1 0 0 -

Can you figure out
the rest?

21b. Special Challenge:
Ode to Joy, Second Part

Start on the D string.

1 1 2 0   1 2 3 2 0

1 2 3 2 1   0 1 **Play this on the G String** 1 -

2 2 3 4   4 3 2 1

0 0 1 2   1 - 0 0

22. Rests

This sign is called a quarter rest:

When you see a rest like this,
stop playing and count to 1
before playing again.

String Class: Play on the
A string or the D string.
Solo: Can be played on all
4 strings.

23. Au clair de la Lune

0 0 0 1 2 ⅃ 1 ⅃

0 2 1 1 0 ⅃ ⅃ ⅃

Repeat

Breaking the notes up

Now we break the notes up with a line: |

String Class: Play on the
D string.
Solo: Can be played on all
4 strings.

24. Purcell's Rigaudon

3 3 2 1 | 0 ⁊ ⁊ ⁊

1 1 2 0 | 3 ⁊ 0 ⁊

3 3 2 1 | 0 ⁊ ⁊ ⁊

1 1 2 0 | 3 ⁊ ⁊ ⁊

25. A Regal March

(on the D String if playing in a class)

0012 | 3322 | 0012 | 1100

0012 | 3322 | 0012 | 1100

26. Three-Leaf Clover

(on the D String if playing in a class)

222 | 012 | 111 | 444

222 | 012 | 111 | 000

333 | 222 | 012 | 111

333 | 222 | 121 | 000

27. Falling Down!
(on the D String if playing in a class)

2210 | 3321 | 2012 | 1 𝄽 1 𝄽

2210 | 3321 | 0211 | 0 𝄽 0 𝄽

28. Waltz
(on the D String if playing in a class)

012 | 333 | 210 | 111

012 | 321 | 232 | 111

012 | 333 | 210 | 111

012 | 333 | 221 | 000

29. Reaching Saturn

(on the D String if playing in a class)

012 | 210 | 123 | 3 𝄽 𝄽

123 | 321 | 234 | 4 𝄽 𝄽

432 | 234 | 321 | 1 𝄽 𝄽

321 | 123 | 210 | 0 𝄽 𝄽

30. Back to Earth

(on the D String if playing in a class)

0210 | 1111 | 1321 | 2222

2012 | 3333 | 2312 | 0000

31. Neptune
(on the D String if playing in a class)

2212 | 3323 | 2212 | 0212﹛

2212 | 3210 | 2232 | 1202﹛

32. Flying Away
(on the D String if playing in a class)

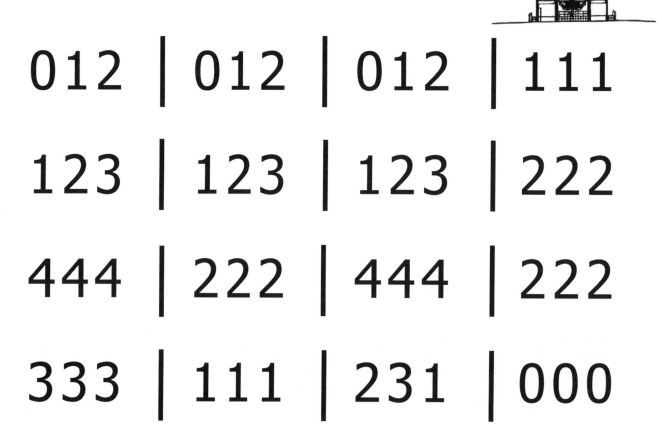

012 | 012 | 012 | 111

123 | 123 | 123 | 222

444 | 222 | 444 | 222

333 | 111 | 231 | 000

33. Reading Music

This is a treble clef sign. The violin plays notes in treble clef.

This is a staff. It has 5 lines and 4 spaces. The notes go on the lines and in the spaces.

The music notes are placed on the lines and in the spaces to mean certain sounds.

Space Notes
Dried
Fish
All
Cats
Enjoy

Line Notes
Every
Good
Boy
Deserves
Fudge

The notes go in order of the alphabet, from A to G, and then start back at A again.

34. Counting

This is a quarter note.
Hold it for 1 count.

This is a half note.
Hold it for 2 counts.

This is a whole note.
Hold it for 4 counts.

This is an eighth note.
Hold it for 1/2 a count.

Two eighth notes
together equal
one quarter note (1 count).

35. A and B on the A String

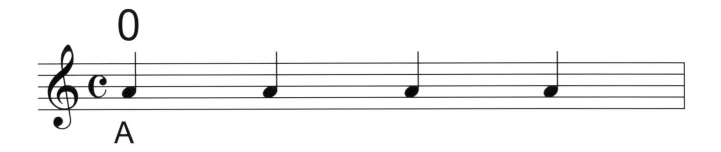

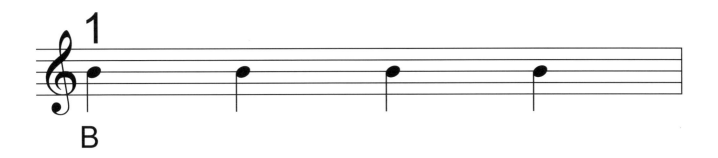

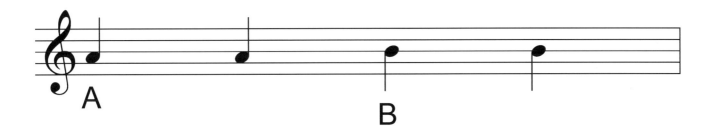

36. A, B, and C♯ on the A String

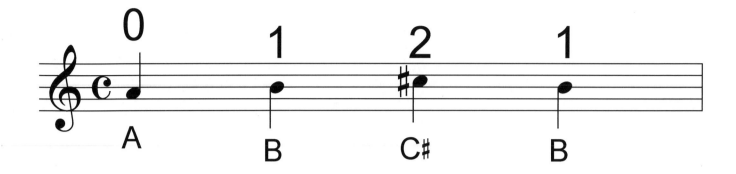

37. A, B, C♯, and D on the A String

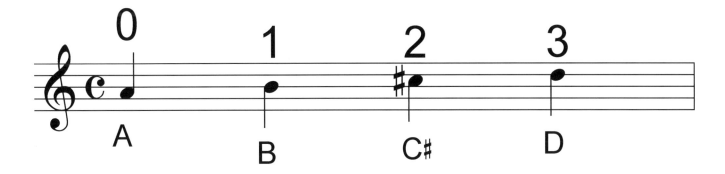

38. Boil Them Cabbage Down

39. Long-Short-Short Cabbage

40. ♩ Half Notes get 2 Counts

41. Mississippi Hot Dogs with Cabbage

42. Miss Mary Mack

43. D and E on the D String

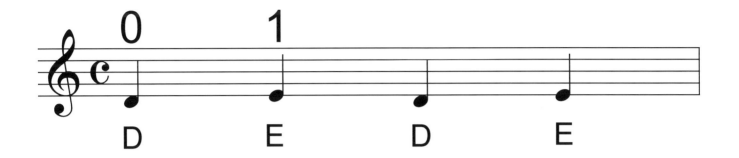

44. D, E, and F♯ on the D String

45. D, E, F♯, and G on the D String

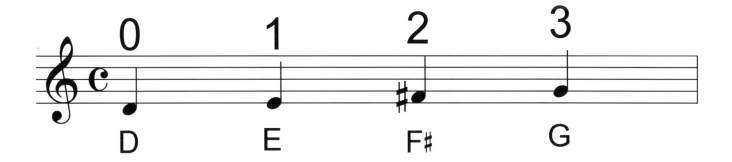

46. Pickle Juice, Pickle Juice

47. Pickle Juice Stomp

48. Peanut Butter Pie Pickle Juice

49. The Rattle Sna-wa-wake

50. The D string and the A string

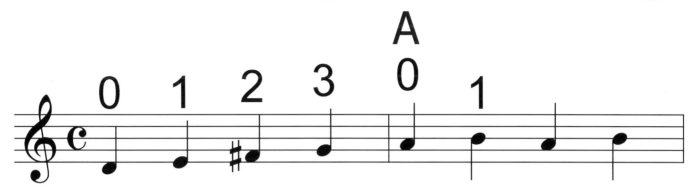

51. Playing on D and A

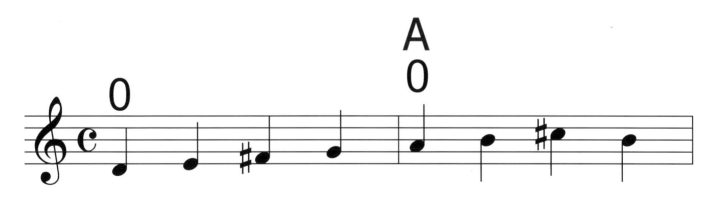

52. Who's That Knocking at my Window?

53. Pounding at the Window!

54. Tapping at the Window!

(Basses learn to shift to 3rd position here.)

55. The D Major Scale

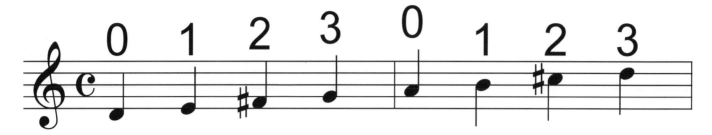

56. Super Challenge!

57. Twinkle, Twinkle, Little Star

58. Twinkle, Twinkle (Mississippi Hot Dog)

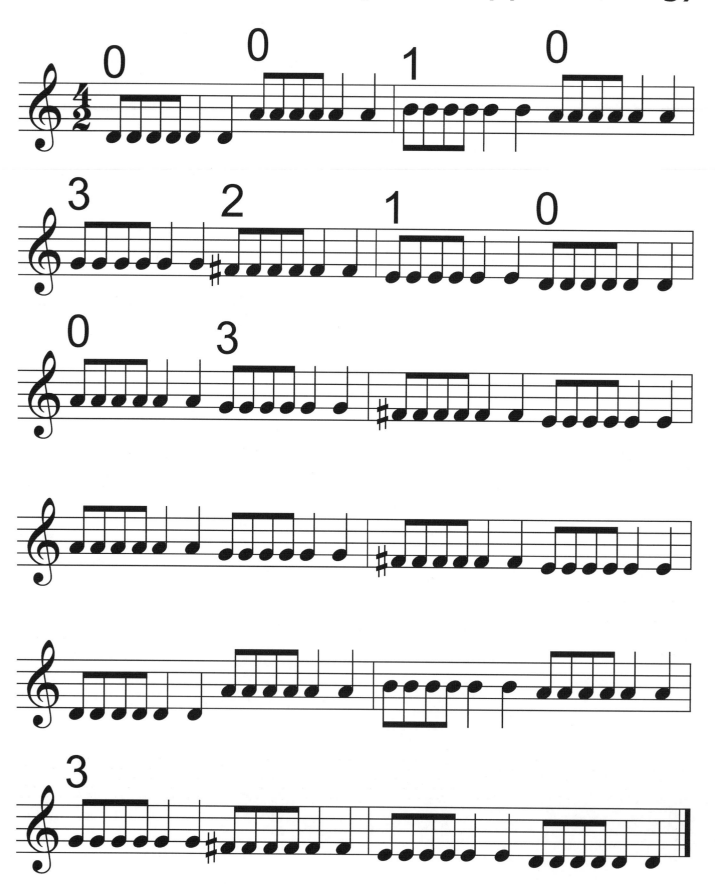

(Basses learn to shift to 3rd position here.)

59. Ode to Joy

Beethoven

First finger on the G string.

60. Fulton Had a Steamboat

61. Pickle Juice Steamboat

62. Blueberry Steamboat

63. Mississippi Hot Dog Steamboat

64. Jingle Bells

65. Dreidel Song

66. The Bears Went Over the Mountain

This note gets
3 counts.

67. Scotland's Burning: A Round

68. Old MacDonald

69. London Bridge

70. Cotton-Eyed Joe

71. Mississippi Hot Dog Joe

72. Blueberry Joe

73. Blueberry Pickle Juice Joe

74. Frere Jacques

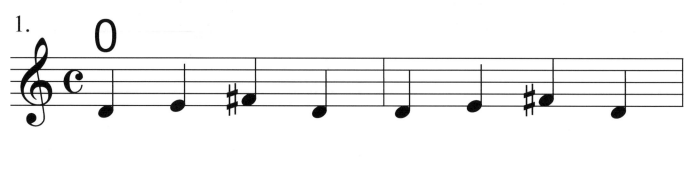

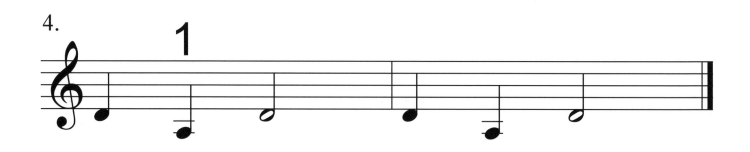

75. E and F# on the E string

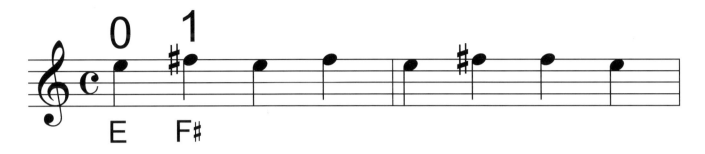

76. E, F#, and G# on the E string

77. E, F#, G#, and A on the E string

78. E, F#, G#, A, and B on the E string

79. The Grey Goose

80. A Goosey Variation

81. Pop Goes the Weasel

82. French Folk Song

83. French Folk Song Harmony
(to play with Violas and Cellos)

84. An Anonymous Allegro

85. G and A on the G String

86. G, A, and B on the G String

87. G, A, B, and C on the G String

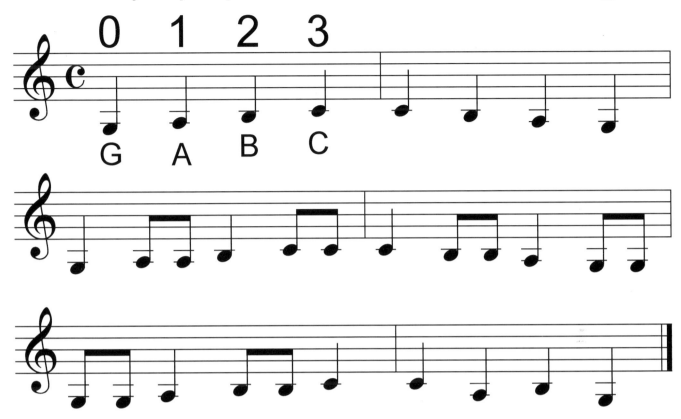

88. G, A, B, C, and D on the G String

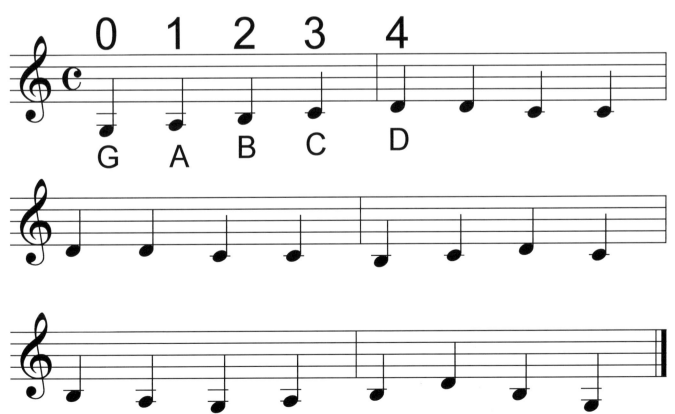

A-hunting we will go, a-hunting we will go

We'll catch a pig and dance a little jig

And then we'll let him go!

89. A-Hunting We Will Go

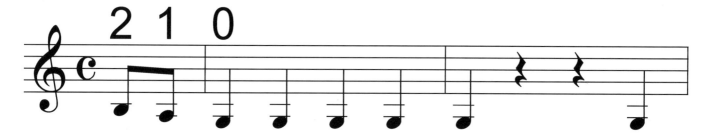

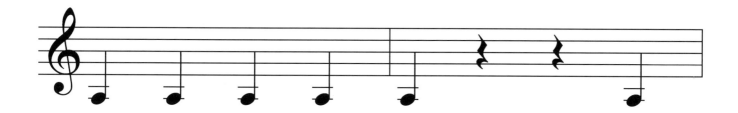

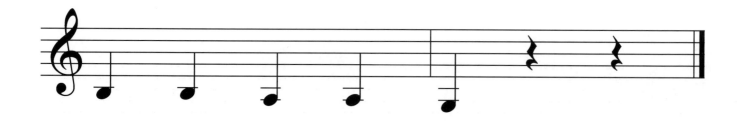

90. River Train

91. Dvorak's Largo

92. Violas and Cellos Learn C and D

93. Violas and Cellos Learn C, D, and E

94. Violas and Cellos Learn C, D, E, and F

95. Violas and Cellos Learn C, D, E, F, and G

96. Hammer Ring

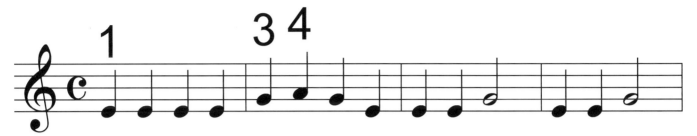

97. Won't You Ring, Old Hammer?

98. Yankee Doodle

99. The Spider Song

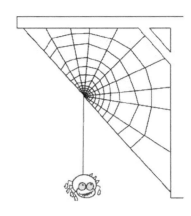

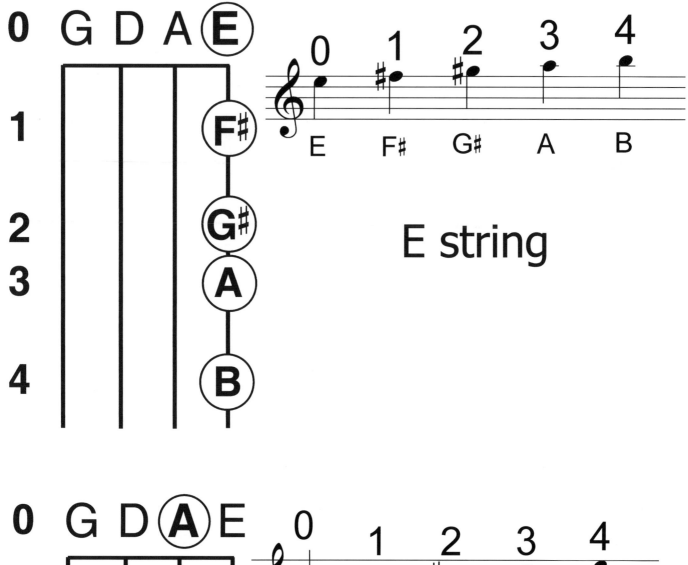

E string

A string

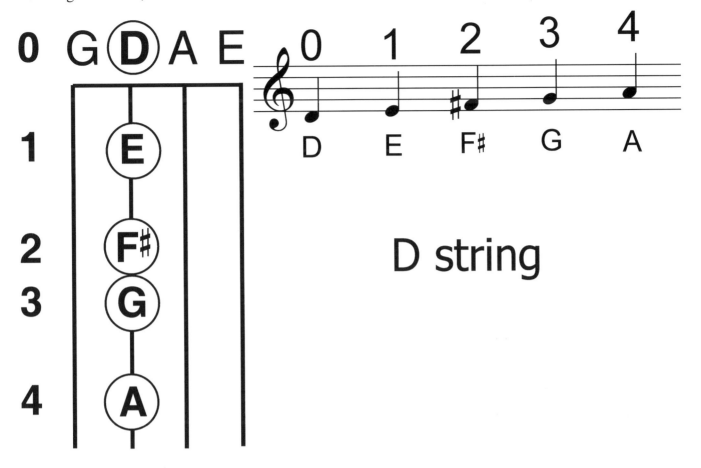

D string

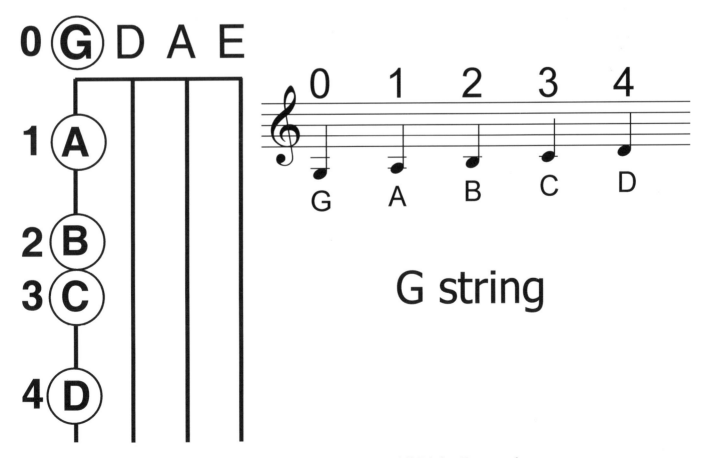

G string

How to Hold the Bow

1. The second (middle) finger covers the sideways "U" section of the frog.

2. The third (ring) finger covers the dot. If your bow does not have a dot, imagine a dot in the very center of the frog.

3. The fourth (pinky) fingertip rests gently on the top of the bow stick, with the finger lightly curved.

4. The first (index) finger rests on its side on the stick, between the first and second knuckles.

5. The thumb bends out slightly and rests on the stick, between the frog and the winding or grip. The thumb should touch the bow where the nail meets the fingertip.

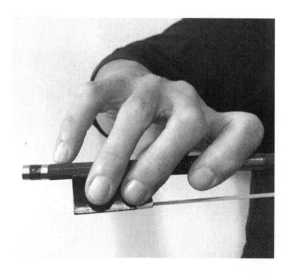

How to Hold the Bow

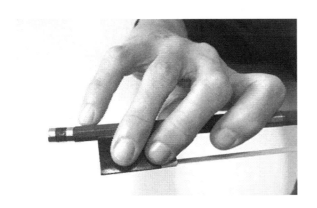

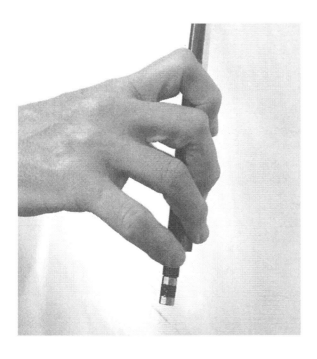

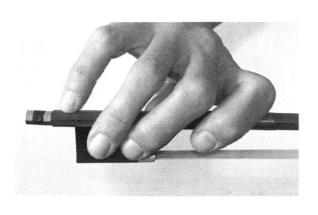

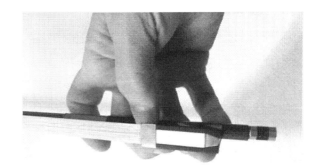

also available from **www.charveypublications.com**

Learning the Violin, Book Two: CHP285

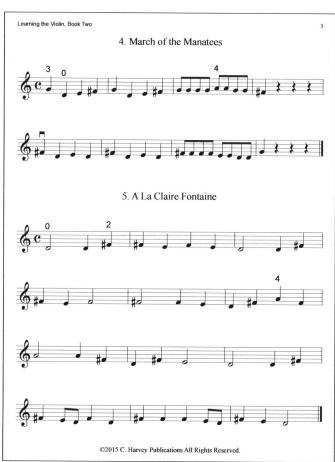

Can be used for
individual study, *single-string classes*,
or *mixed-string classes*, with:

Learning the Viola, Book Two: CHP286

Learning the Cello, Book Two: CHP287

Learning the Bass, Book Two: CHP288

Learning the Violin, Viola, Cello, and Bass, Book Two, Score: CHP289

also available from **www.charveypublications.com**

Playing the Violin, Book One: CHP298

Can be used for
individual study, *single-string classes*,
or *mixed-string classes*, with:

Playing the Viola, Book One: CHP299

Playing the Cello, Book One: CHP300

Playing the Bass, Book One: CHP301

Playing the Violin, Viola, Cello, and Bass, Book One, Score: CHP302

Supplemental Books for Learning the Violin, Book One

The Open-String Book for Violin
Short open-string studies for the beginning violinist. CHP249 $9

The Hot Cross Buns Book for Violin
50 variations on Hot Cross Buns for the beginning violinist. CHP154 $9

The A-String Book for Violin
Learn the notes on the A string on the violin with short exercises and pieces. CHP213 $9

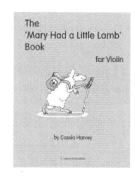

The 'Mary Had a Little Lamb' Book for Violin
50 variations on Mary Had a Little Lamb for the beginning violinist. CHP168 $9

The D-String Book for Violin
Learn the notes on the D string on the violin with short exercises and pieces. CHP240 $9

Early Exercises for the Violin
Very easy exercises for beginning violinists. CHP292 $9

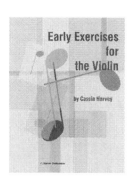

Beginning Fiddle Duets for Two Violins, Book One
Fun and easy fiddle and folk duets for beginning violinists. Includes Old Joe Clark, Cripple Creek and more. CHP303 $9

All books are available from www.charveypublications.com, at online retailers, or through your local music store.

Other First-Position Violin Books from C. Harvey Publications

Double Stop Beginnings for Violin, Book One
A method for learning double stops on the violin. CHP247 $9

Double Stop Beginnings for Violin, Book Two
The second book in a double stop method for violin. CHP248 $9

The First Summer Study Book for Violin
Exercises and short pieces to learn for fun. CHP186 $9

Finger Exercises for the Violin, Book One
Violin finger training in first position for intonation and agility. CHP185 $9

Finger Exercises for the Violin, Book Two
Further violin finger training in first position for intonation and agility. CHP266 $9

Flying Fiddle Duets for Two Violins, Book One
Fun and exciting duets in first position for two violins. CHP263 $10

Flying Fiddle Duets for Two Violins, Book Two
A continuation of the fun series of fiddle duets for two violins. CHP307 $10

Knowing the Notes for Violin
Short exercises & pieces to help with violin note reading. CHP132 $9

Playing in Keys for Violin, Book One
Study the keys of C, G, and D major on the violin. CHP254 $9

Playing the Violin, Book Two
Exercises and short pieces for second-year violin study. CHP169 $9

Playing the Violin, Book Three
Exercises and short pieces for third-year violin study. CHP225 $9

The Triplet Book for Violin, Part One
Studies and short fiddle tunes to practice triplets on the violin. CHP267 $10

**All books are available from www.charveypublications.com,
at online retailers, or through your local music store.**

Other Intermediate and Advanced Violin Books
from C. Harvey Publications

Fourth Position for the Violin
A method for learning fourth position on the violin. CHP246 $10

G Major Shifting for the Violin
Shifting to second, third, and fourth position in G major. CHP257 $9

Getting in Shape for Violin
Easy warm-ups for violinists or string classes. CHP123 $9

Octave Scale Studies for the Violin, Book One
A set of octave double stop studies for the advanced violinist. CHP262 $9

Octaves for the Violin, Book One
A method for learning octave double stops for the intermediate violinist. CHP166 $9

Scale Studies (One String) for the Violin, Part One
Scale variations for the intermediate violinist. CHP178 $9

Second Position for the Violin
A method for learning second position on the violin. CHP253 $9

Serial Shifting for the Violin
Shifting exercises in rows and patterns for the violin. CHP195 $9

Shifting in Keys for Violin, Book One
Violin shifting studies in the keys of C, G, D, F, and B- at major. CHP256 $9

Third Position for the Violin, Book One
A method for learning third position on the violin. CHP196 $9

Third Position Study Book for the Violin, Book One
Short exercises and pieces that train the violinist to play in third position. CHP217 $9

The Two Octaves Book for Violin
Major and minor scales, broken thirds, and arpeggios, with numerous bowing and rhythm
variations, in two octaves for the violin. CHP265 $10

Warming Up for Violin, Book One
Warm up on the violin with exercises and short pieces.
Can be used for individual study, single-string classes, or mixed-string classes. CHP118 $9

Warming Up for Violin, Book Two
Warm up on the violin with exercises and short pieces.
Can be used for individual study, single-string classes, or mixed-string classes. CHP146 $9

**All books are available from www.charveypublications.com,
at online retailers, or through your local music store.**

Made in the USA
San Bernardino, CA
26 February 2020